Rooo!

Nancy Hassell

Hunk

PROUD RACER

One Greyhound's Journey

by

Nancy A. Lassiter

PENMAN PUBLISHING, INC.

First Published 2002
Penman Publishing, Inc.
4159 Ringgold Road, Suite 104
Chattanooga, Tennessee 37412

PROUD RACER
One Greyhound's Journey

by
Nancy A. Lassiter

ISBN: 0-9720775-2-9

Photographs courtesy of Scott I. Lassiter

Manufactured in the United States of America.

Printed by Penman Publishing, Inc.

This book is dedicated to:

The Nice Lady, Loretta Steed, for taking care of the precious lives of the greyhounds on her farm... especially Hunkamuncha from Oz...

As well as my foster hounds, Foxi-Roxi Hart, Striper, Abee-Babee, Xena-Beena, Bogey, Buddy, Dori, Bucky-Loo, Onyx-Phonyx, Darcie, Nelly-Belly, Carrie, Marky, Luna-Tuna, Skitzy, and especially Henry, for teaching me about loving and letting go...

And most definitely, the thousands of greyhounds that sadly never find the true reward of being a Proud Racer...

PROUD RACER

One Greyhound's Journey

The puppy was born in Florida. It was warm and sunny there, and the puppy loved playing in the sun with his brothers and sisters on the farm. There was a Nice Lady there with long, curly hair who took extra good care of all the pups, and the puppy loved her. She called him "puppy-puppy," and he danced whenever he heard her voice.

His life was happy and carefree, until the day he turned three months old. That was when he got his name. His momma had told him in hushed tones at night that one day he would be a great Racer, just like his daddy; but the puppy didn't understand what a Racer was, and he had never met his daddy. One sunny morning, the Nice Lady came into the pen where the puppy and his brothers and sisters were playing, and she had a man with her who was carrying a funny looking metal thing. The puppy cocked his head to one side to get a better look.

"Now, puppies, let's get this done and you can be on your way to being champs," the Nice Lady said. The puppy was puzzled. *Champs? I thought we were going to be Racers!* His thoughts were interrupted by the sound of one of his brothers yelping loudly. His head spun around, and he saw the Nice Lady holding another of his brothers and wiping some green stuff on his ears. Maybe it was like the squirty medicine they all got last week? The puppy's eyes widened as the man clamped something metal down on his brother's ear, and the pup yelped. The puppy cowered behind another pup as the Nice Lady came for him.

"Come here, puppy, it's not so bad," she said, and the puppy's fear melted a bit. The Nice Lady had never hurt him; why would this be different? His brother was just a wuss. The puppy carefully came to her, and she scooped him up, scratching him behind the ears. "Be careful with this one," she said, "because his ears are sensitive and I don't want to get bitten." The puppy licked her hands, trying to let her know that he would never bite her.

"What's this one's name?" the man asked the Nice Lady.

"Um, Fond A Hunk," she said, turning the puppy over and inspecting him. The man wrote something on a piece of paper as the Nice Lady started wiping the green stuff in the puppy's ears. "We'll call him Hunk, as a kennel name," she said. The puppy wrinkled his nose. *Hunk?* What kind of name was that? "Okay, I'm ready," she said.

The man came over with the metal thing. "This one is the 'D' pup," he said, placing the metal thing over Hunk's ear. Hunk braced himself as the man squeezed the metal thing. It felt like a swarm of bees all stinging Hunk's ear at the same time. He squealed. Maybe his brother wasn't such a wuss after all!

"There now, hush, little Hunk," the Nice Lady said. "Just one more ear and you're done."

ONE MORE! Hunk wiggled and squirmed, trying to get away. He didn't want to bite the Nice Lady, but that really hurt and now...OW! The man had sneaked up on him and stung his other ear.

As suddenly as it had happened, however, the pain was gone. The Nice Lady put Hunk back on the ground and started for one of his sisters. Hunk stumbled over to the brother that had been pinched right before him. "Hey, what did they name you?" he asked.

Hunk's brother looked at him funny. "Name me?" he asked. "What do you mean? They just pinched me, looked at my feet, and put me back down."

"You mean they didn't give you a weird name?" Hunk asked.

"No. The Nice Lady kept telling me I was remarkable, but that my feet were wrong." The puppy hung his head. "Guess I'm not gonna be a Racer like Momma told us."

Hunk's eyes brightened. "Do you know what a Racer is?" he asked.

"Not really," his brother answered. "Just that it's the greatest thing and I think you get to run a lot."

"Huh." Hunk plopped down into the cool dirt to think. His brother paced about, looking nervous. "So, do you want a name?" he asked.

The puppy looked down at his brother. "I

guess so. Maybe my name is Remarkable, because that's what the Nice Lady kept saying."

"That's too long," Hunk said. "My name is Fond A Hunk, but she said they'd call me Hunk for short."

The other puppy nearly fell to the ground laughing. "Hunk?" he said through his puppy giggles. "That's the most ridiculous name I've ever heard!"

Hunk glared at his brother. "At least I have a name!" he said, instantly regretting his words when he saw a profoundly sad look come over his brother's face. "Remarkable, huh? Maybe we can shorten it? To Marky?"

A twinkle appeared in the pup's eyes. "Marky?" he said. "Marky. I like it. I'm Marky!!!" He danced off after a bee, leaving Hunk to doze in the sun.

Shortly after that, a buzz of gossip swept through the puppy pens. Some of them were going to go Away to become Racers. Hunk couldn't wait! He had learned from some of the other Mama-dogs that his daddy was a famous Racer named Fond A Hulk, and that the people really loved Hulk. Hunk wanted to be just like his daddy, whom he still had not met.

The day came for the pups to go Away, and Hunk could hardly wait. He had seen this happen before, with the pups that were several months older than he was. A huge white truck came and all the pups were loaded into it. Hunk wasn't sure where Away was, or what would happen there, but he knew he wanted to make the Nice Lady proud so that she would love him like she loved Hulk. The man and the Nice Lady came into the puppy pen and started putting leashes on some of the pups. Hunk was there with his brothers, Tony and Marky, and his sisters, Totem, Roo, and Tawny, and all of them danced around the Nice Lady's feet.

Suddenly Hunk noticed that they were being led out to the truck, and that Marky was still in the pen. Hunk pulled on his leash to let the Nice Lady know that she had forgotten Marky, but she just kept leading him on to the truck. "Come on Hunk-amuncha from Oz," she said, great affection in her voice. "No time to be lazy now. You'll have plenty of time for that in the hauler."

Hunk tugged on his leash and even yipped a few times, but the Nice Lady just kept on until she had lifted poor Hunk into the truck with the others. In the meantime, Marky was barking and rooing and trying to get the Nice Lady's attention, but she never went back for him.

"Marky!" Hunk screamed as loudly as he could. "We'll see you when we get back! Don't worry!" Marky was still barking and rooing as though his heart was about to break. "I love you, bro!" Hunk yelled as the people shut the door to the hauler.

"I won't forget you, Hunk," Marky yelled back, then sat down on the dirt to cry.

A lot happened for Hunk during training. He didn't really know where he was, only that he was Away, and some of the people called what he was doing "Schooling." There were nice people at Away who taught Hunk how to run in a straight line, how to follow the little stuffy thing, which they called a Rabbit, as it raced around the dirt circle, and how to run really fast. Hunk remembered playing a similar game with the Nice Lady, and how she had run around his pen with a mop, letting him and his brothers chase it.

Now and then Hunk thought of Marky, but the longer Hunk was Away, the more his memories of Marky began to fade. He didn't see his other brother and sisters much anymore either, but made new friends at Schooling.

Finally Hunk was ready for the next step, according to the people at Schooling. The next step was something called the Track, and Hunk didn't really know what it was but was eager as always to go. Maybe the Nice Lady would be there, and he could show her everything he had learned at Schooling! The day came when the white truck again was parked outside the kennel, and Hunk was loaded on and into a crate. He could hardly stand the ride, he was so anxious to get back and see the Nice Lady again.

When the truck finally stopped, Hunk woke from his nap to unfamiliar smells. Where were they? It was hot, like Home with the Nice Lady, but it smelled wrong. The people put a leash on him and led him out of the truck. There was a kennel building there, sort of like the one at Home, but not as big. Hunk didn't recognize any of the dogs there, and he felt afraid for the first time since he had left Home for Away. He wanted to run for the Nice Lady, so that she would scratch him behind the ears and call him Hunkamuncha from Oz. Hunk hung his head and let the people lead him into a crate. He winced as he heard the latch lock, and then he lay down to go back to sleep.

Hunk slept most of the night. He was awakened now and again to the whimpers of other dogs near him. There was a thunderstorm that night, and some of the pups that hadn't come from his Home had never seen this kind of storm. Hunk whispered to them that it would be all right and it would pass, and some of them settled down. One pup in a cage close to his, however, wasn't calming down.

"Hey," Hunk called out, trying to keep his voice low. "Hey, what's your name?" he asked.

The frightened dog raised his head. "Bob," he said. "T's Casino Bob. Who are you?"

"Hunk. Fond A Hunk," Hunk whispered proudly. "Don't worry, Bob, it's just a storm and it will go away." Bob shook his head and continued to whimper. "Just think about tomorrow, Bob," Hunk said as reassuringly as he could. He tried to think back on those nights with his mother in what the Nice Lady called the Momma-House. He remembered her shushing one of his brothers who was terribly afraid of the thunder. "It's just noise," Hunk whispered. "There's nothing behind it. Think, tomorrow we become Racers!" Hunk held his head up and looked around the kennel. "Some of us here already are Racers."

"Ssssh!" said one of the older dogs. "Keep that up and you won't be doing anything tomorrow but what you're doing now!"

Hunk hung his head. He wanted to apologize to the older dog for being noisy, but wasn't sure who had shushed him. He laid his head down on his paws and closed his eyes.

"Pssst! Hunk!" said Bob.

"Yeah?" Hunk whispered.

"Thanks. I hope you win tomorrow," Bob said, a slight tremor of fear remaining in his voice. Hunk smiled, then drifted back to sleep.

The next morning, Hunk discovered he

For the next month and a half, Hunk raced at Seminole. He tried his best each time, and almost won one of his races. The dogs around him came and went. New dog trucks arrived and new faces filled the kennel. One day, however, when the dog truck came, one of the people came to his crate, took him out, and snapped a leash on him. "Time to move on, Boy," the person said, walking him toward the truck. Hunk panicked. What was happening? He knew he hadn't won any races, but he was still a Racer, wasn't he? He whined a bit as he was latched into his cage in the hauler and then settled down, expecting a long ride like the one from Away to Seminole.

Hunk awoke unexpectedly when the hauler stopped. He lifted his head and sniffed. Home? Could it really be? He scrambled to his feet, and excitedly hopped up and down with his front feet until his turn came to be let out of the hauler. Sure enough, when he looked around outside, he was Home. The pens, the pups, the Momma-House...and the Nice Lady. Hunk pulled and tugged at his leash, trying to break free and run to her.

"Hunkamuncha from Oz!" she exclaimed, holding her arms out as she squatted down next to him. He licked her face happily, and put his long nose into her curly hair. *Home*, he thought. *I'm home.*

As he and the other dogs were being led away from the hauler, he noticed that they were not going back to the puppy pens. Hunk tugged on his leash, trying to tell the Nice Lady that she was going the wrong way.

"Oh, no, Hunkamuncha," she said, laughing. "You're a little too big to play with the puppies." *Too big?* Hunk thought. He knew he had gotten taller, but didn't know that he was now two years old, and that it had been a year and a half since he left Home. He was going to the kennel building where the older dogs lived! As they got close to the gate, Hunk noticed a dog standing near the building, surveying the crowd about to enter the gate. The dog was a reddish brindle like Hunk, but had a white stripe around his neck. His feet were completely flat, and when he scampered toward the gate he sort of resembled a duck in gait. Hunk cocked his head to one side, trying to get a better look at this dog.

"Hunk?" the dog called out. This dog knew his name! "Hunk? It's me, Marky!" said the dog as he happily charged toward Hunk. Hunk took a step back, unsure of this dog. The name was familiar, but the face was wrong. Hunk sniffed deeply and suddenly caught the scent of his mother on this dog. This was one of his brothers! Hunk and Marky danced around happily, reacquainting themselves. *This must be the reward for being a Racer*, Hunk thought, *getting to come back Home*.

His time at Home was short, though. After about a month and a half, the dogs started talking about the hauler coming, and that some of them were going to a place called Melbourne. Hunk began to get excited. Perhaps this Melbourne place was like Seminole, and he could run every night! Maybe the Nice Lady could even see him run! She had not been around as much lately as she was when he was a puppy, but he still wanted to make her proud.

Sure enough, when the hauler arrived, Hunk was one of the dogs loaded up. The trip was the same, and once again Hunk had to say good-bye to his brother Marky. "I'll see you soon," he had whispered to Marky that morning before Turn-Out. "The reward for Racers is to come back Home, so I'll be back soon." Marky nodded, not smiling.

"What if you forget me again, Hunk?" Marky asked.

"I won't forget you, silly," Hunk said. "You're my brother, and we'll always end up together. You wait and see." As the hauler pulled away from Home, Hunk again settled down to sleep with dreams of being a Racer filling his head.

This time the racing was a little bit different. It was later in the year, and colder, so the Handlers would move the dogs in and out of the kennel building faster to keep them warm. Hunk never did like to rush around unless he was racing, so he got snapped at more than a few times to hurry up. Each time he would hang his head, wishing he were back Home with Marky.

Just as before, the longer he was away, the faster his memory of Marky faded. It was only after he had been at Melbourne for five months and Seminole for a month that he got to return home for a month because it was too hot to race. He and Marky had barely said hello this time when the hauler came to take Hunk back to race. This time, he ended up at Seminole again, back where he had started.

It was fun to run on the track again that was so familiar. Hunk met lots of new dogs; some he raced against and some he just saw in the kennel. He was getting weighed before a race that August when he heard a familiar female bark. Hunk scanned the row of dogs being dressed out in silks and checked for proper tattoo numbers. There, standing in the group, was a little fawn female that he recognized from Home. Clips! Her racing name was Little Clips, and he had met her on his first reward trip back home. He tried to go over and say hello, but his handler tightened his grip on Hunk's leash.

"None of that, Boy," the Handler said. "You can play with the ladies when you win a lot of races."

Play with the Ladies? Hunk thought. He

didn't know what that meant, only that he wanted to say hello to Clips before they got put in the boxes. Oh well...

Hunk continued racing, winning a few here and there, but he never again left Seminole for a new track. Late at night he would hear the other dogs talking about other places like Daytona Beach and Jacksonville, and a tiny little track called Ebro. Hunk thought he must be pretty good, because they let him stay at Seminole, until he mentioned that to one of the older dogs.

The older dog laughed. "You stay here because you're a loser," he sneered, and Hunk hung his head. "You have to win races to go to other tracks. You're staying here because you're slow."

"You don't go to other tracks if you win, stupid," Hunk jeered back. "You get to play with the Ladies. I heard the Handlers say so."

At this, several of the older dogs roared. "You don't know anything about the world outside of that cage, do you?" said another one. "If you win and win, you move around a lot and then you get to go to the farm and make puppies." Hunk cocked his head to one side. How could *he* make puppies? The girl dogs did that. If he didn't win, was he going to become a girl? He didn't dare voice *that* question.

"But if you lose," chimed in another dog, "and lose a lot, as you've been doing, you go away and don't come back."

Hunk spun around to face that voice. "Wwhh-where do you go?" he stammered. "Home?"

The kennel fell silent, for not even the older dogs knew the answer. "We don't know," said one finally. "All we know is that some of us leave and don't come back. I've heard talk of dogs being Petted Out, but I don't know what that means." Hunk swallowed hard. It sounded like if you didn't win, they would just shove you out into the night, like being left accidentally in the turnout pen all alone.

"Then I have to start winning!" Hunk said. There was silence. "If I win, I won't get Petted Out, right?" Still there was no answer. "Do you know something?"

Finally one of the dogs directly across from Hunk raised his head. His name was Jared, and

Hunk had just raced against him that afternoon. "We're leaving tonight, Hunk, all of us that are Ds are leaving," Jared said. "I've heard we're going to the Farm, but I have no idea what that means."

"I don't want to go to the Farm," Hunk stammered, trying to keep back tears. "I want to stay here. I want to run and race."

Jared's voice was low but comforting. "It will be all right, Hunk. You're the son of the famous Fond A Hulk. Don't forget that." Hunk hung his head. "Pick your head up, Boy," Jared said, trying to imitate the Handlers as they gave the dogs pep talks before the parade. "Act like the Proud Racer you are." Hunk raised his eyes to look at Jared, then turned around three times and settled into his bedding.

Hunk felt as though he had just shut his eyes when the people came to load him into the truck. He thought for a moment about fighting them and running back to the security of his crate, but he didn't. *Act like the Proud Racer you are*, he thought. He held his head high and hopped up into the hauler as he was told. As he closed his eyes in his crate, he hoped that when he opened them this would all have been a dream, and that he would be safe and warm at Home, waiting for another white truck and another trip to a Track.

The jolting of the hauler as the truck came to a stop awakened Hunk. He lifted his head and took a deep breath, hoping to figure out where they were. He shook his head to clear it. He had to be wrong. That was the smell of Home! Hunk raised his ears to listen carefully, and to his sheer delight he heard the familiar voice of the Nice Lady outside the hauler. He rooed with glee, and soon the other dogs joined in the song. The hauler doors opened, and he was taken out into the sunshine. Hunk danced toward the Nice Lady. "Hunkamuncha, back again I see?" she said, and he eagerly licked her face when she bent over to scratch him.

Marky was still there, and had gotten even taller since Hunk saw him last. Hunk remembered him, and they played and romped as though no time had passed. Another hauler came, and Hunk noticed a dog he had met at Melbourne in the kennel...Henry. Henry had raced as Fine Henry, and had won a lot of races before his accident. After that, he just wasn't fast enough. Hunk had feared the worst when Henry was taken Away, but he was overjoyed to see his friend now. There were other familiar faces to be greeted: Striper, a red male with a white stripe on the back of his neck who was a bit older than Hunk but still liked to play; Onyx, a stunning black male who came and went frequently and always seemed just a bit too full of himself; and Skitzy, who lived up to his name and was limping around as his leg healed from the break that ended his racing career.

Hunk was in heaven! This was the best reward yet! Old friends, new faces... Hunk wanted to stay at Home forever. But, as was every other trip to Home, this one was to be short. After a few months at Home, Hunk was at Turn-Out when the Nice Lady came toward the pen with two leashes. The dogs all looked at one another, wondering whom she would pick. Hunk nearly danced with joy when she came to him and clipped the leash onto his collar. He was going to race again! Those old dogs at the track were wrong!

"I can't believe this day has come,

Hunkamuncha!" she said. *I know*, Hunk thought, *I thought I was done with racing!* "You're going to make someone a wonderful pet though, big sweet marshmallow boy like you."

What? *Pet*? Was this the dreaded *Petting Out* that he had heard about at the track? What was happening? Hunk wrenched his head around to look over his shoulder at the pen. The man who was always with the Nice Lady had come out of the pen with Henry on a leash.

Suddenly Hunk knew what was happening. He had heard rumors, of course, that sometimes when dogs were hurt they went somewhere and were never seen again. He wracked his brain and was unhappily greeted with a memory from his puppy days...one of his brothers had been born unable to walk, and they had taken him away. The other pups talked about how being taken away was awful, and that you never come back. Surely the Nice Lady wasn't going to do that to him! Hunk strained on his leash now, trying desperately to break free and get back to the pen.

"Hunkamuncha," the Nice Lady said, in that voice that made him stop in his tracks.

"Come on now, it won't be so bad. I know the truck is small, but you'll be all right." Hunk swung his head around and saw that she was leading him to their truck, and not to a hauler. He hung his head and let her lead him. Just as he was about to get into the truck, he heard a strong bark from a pen nearby. He raised his head to see a magnificent brindle male standing there, watching him.

"Act like the Proud Racer you are, boy," said the male. "I won't have any son of mine walking with his head down like a loser." Hunk's eyes widened and he stopped in his tracks. He was staring at Fond a Hulk, the famous Racer. His father.

"Come on, Hunk," urged the Nice Lady. "Now is not the time to get sentimental over leaving your Pop over there." It was true! Hunk raised his head high as he had for so many parades, and continued toward the truck.

"Atta boy," said Hulk. "Be a good Pet, Son. It's not so bad."

Soon, Hunk was joined in the truck by Henry, and then by a little fawn girl that he didn't know very well. "What's your name?"

he asked her.

She looked up at him, her big eyes wide and fearful. "Jeany," she said, "Where are we going? Is it cleaner? I hope so. At Jacksonville it was always clean and the lights were bright. What's your name? Are you brothers?"

Boy, Hunk thought, *I bet she got in trouble for being noisy a lot at the Track.* "I'm Hunk," he said, "and this is Henry." Henry raised his head, studied Jeany for a moment, and then lowered it again as he sighed dismissively. "You'll have to excuse Henry," Hunk explained. "He's old." Jeany giggled. "Where's Jacksonville?" Hunk asked.

"I don't know," Jeany replied. "Only that's where I raced and I didn't like it because I wanted to play and every time I played they would fuss at me because I wasn't doing it right and there were bright lights there and it was clean." She paused, licking her nose with her pink tongue. "My grandpa was named Dutch Bahama and he ran really fast and I'm a Bahama GrandBaby but I don't know what that means but I have his eyes because they're dark underneath." She turned around a few times and then settled into her seat. "I'm sleepy and I'm hungry and when are they going to let us out of here?"

Hunk sighed. He hoped the trip would be short, because the thought of listening to her ramble for a long trip was not pleasant. "Soon, now go to sleep," he said. He turned around his customary three times, then settled down to sleep.

At long last the Nice Lady and the man stopped the truck and unloaded Hunk, Henry, and Jeany. Hunk took a deep breath, but once again, the smell was unfamiliar. There were other dogs around, though. The Nice Lady was talking to another woman who had big eyes that seemed to dance when she talked. The woman came over to him and knelt down in front of him.

"So you're the famous Hunkamuncha?" she asked, taking his nose in her hand. Hunk jerked his head back, staring at her in disbelief. *Famous? Like my Daddy?* The woman laughed, and Hunk found that her laugh sounded happy and warm like the Nice Lady's. The woman then went to Henry and Jeany and was introduced. Hunk was too tired to look around much, and was grateful to be loaded into a crate for the night.

The next morning when he awoke, Hunk wasn't sure where he was. The trip the night before was hazy in his memory now, and all he knew was that he was very hungry. Another woman had brought him some food, but it didn't smell right and it was hard, like pebbles. He wasn't going to eat that, for sure! Henry seemed very happy to see the woman, and he told Hunk later that this woman had helped with some of his Schooling. Jeany was still sleeping, so Hunk settled down to wait for Turn Out.

Turn Out came, but instead of being led around or let out in a pen, Hunk found himself being loaded into a van along with Henry. Were they leaving Jeany? Hunk called out to her as they left the kennel, and heard her begin to wail when she realized she was alone. The sound hurt his ears and his heart. *Poor little thing. She'll get used to moving around soon enough*, he thought.

When the van finally stopped and the woman took Hunk and Henry out, Hunk found himself back at the place where they had made the stop the night before. The same laughing woman with the big beautiful eyes was there, along with another woman and man who were staring at him. Hunk was unsure and hung back behind Henry. Whatever was going to happen, let it happen to Henry first!

Hunk heard the women introducing him and Henry to the two newcomers. Henry went straight for the man and sniffed him all over, wagging his tail. The woman came toward Hunk and knelt down to look at him. Gathering his courage, he walked over to her to sniff her as he had seen Henry do. She smelled wonderful, like sunflowers and soap and…was that cheeseburger? Her voice was soft and she looked as though she might cry. Finally she said his name. "Hunk?" He looked up at her and she laughed with delight. She walked around the yard with him, holding his leash and talking to him, and sometimes just looking at him. Hunk couldn't explain it, but he really liked this lady, almost as much as the Nice

Lady. "Can I be your Momma?" the lady asked him. Hunk cocked his head to one side. He already had a Momma...didn't he? It was so hard to remember. The lady looked sort of lost, so Hunk walked over and licked her face. Again, the lady laughed happily, and Hunk knew he had done the right thing.

After a while, the man and woman left, and Hunk was still there with Henry. He went back to the kennel with Henry, but that night the two boys were to be taken away again, leaving Jeany alone. The little fawn girl wept bitterly before they left.

"I don't like being alone," she wailed.

"Don't worry," Hunk said. "I used to be upset when I'd leave a Track, but I always saw my friends again. Don't cry. I just know I'll see you again." He thought for a moment, then licked her face through the crate bars. "Your grandpa was an important dog, and so are you," he told her. "Act like the Proud Racer you are."

She smiled at him as the kennel door shut, and Hunk was still smiling as he was being loaded into the van. He didn't know where he was going this time, but he knew it would turn out okay, as long as he held his head high and acted like the Proud Racer he had been, just like his Daddy had told him.

Hunk woke up when he heard the New Lady call his name. It was getting dark, and he wasn't sure where he was for a moment. The past week had been a bit of a blur. There was a trip to the vet, which Hunk had experienced plenty of times before, but this time the vet made him take a nap... and when he woke up, his teeth felt funny and there was a sharp pain in his back end every time he walked. He had been sleeping most of the week, with short Turn Outs and more of that strange pebble food.

"Come on, you sleepy head," the New Lady said. Her big eyes sparkled. Something good must be coming! Hunk had learned that people only get that look in their eyes when treats or a race is coming. He had long since given up on going back to racing, however, because he knew now that he was a Pet...whatever that meant. "Your new Momma and Daddy will be here to get you soon."

Hunk's eyes flew open wide. *New Momma and Daddy?* he thought. *I already have a Momma and Daddy...don't I?* He racked his brain, and was horrified when he couldn't remember what his Momma looked like, or her smell, or any of that. He did what the New Lady told him to do, though still trying to remember. The only images that came to him were of Marky watching him from behind the fence and of his father, Hulk...and so Hunk held his head up tall, just as his father had instructed. The New Lady laughed.

"Why, Hunkamuncha, if I didn't know better I'd swear you thought you were going to the race!" she said, smiling and stroking his head gently. She was so good to him, just like the Nice Lady at Home. Hunk hoped that wherever he was going she would be going also, because she somehow made him feel safe. He licked her face and then danced about happily.

The New Lady had gotten Henry out of his crate while Hunk was dancing about. Henry scowled slightly at Hunk. Apparently the nap that he had at the vet was not good like Hunk's, and he'd been complaining ever since. He'd also been eyeballing the New Lady's cat, Cleo, and whispering to Hunk at night about how yummy cats are. Hunk had never even considered such a thing! After all, the New Lady seemed to love Cleo, and Cleo smelled so interesting...and her fur was so soft. Hunk didn't want to eat her; he wanted to play with her and find out what a CAT is.

"Listen," Henry had whispered to Hunk one night, "I heard the New Lady and the Robert talking, and it seems there are more of these," he nodded toward the cat, who was quietly resting on the arm of the chair next to the New Lady, "at the New Home where we're going!" Hunk cocked his head to one side and stared back at Henry.

"I'm not sure what you mean," Hunk said. "So what? The New Home is crowded?"

Henry rolled his eyes. "You are a young one, aren't you? Lots of these things means no more pebble food! If we're good, then maybe we can have them instead!"

Hunk's eyes widened in shock. "We're not supposed to eat them, Henry!" he said, outdone. "The New Lady has told us that again and again! Don't you understand, if we eat them, then we go where the Used Up Racers went from the track? We have to be good and do what the New Lady says! She loves us!"

Henry laughed full and hard at Hunk, leaving Hunk mortified. He puffed out his cheeks, waiting for Henry to tell him how stupid he was. Instead, however, Henry merely looked at Hunk, tears running down his cheeks from the laughter. "Hunk," he said, "you're going to be a good Pet. I'll make a deal with you. I'll give the New Home a few months, and I won't eat the Cats. I'll try my best." Hunk again cocked his head to one side.

"Why?" he asked, genuinely confused.

"Because you're my Brother now. The New Lady said so." Henry hung his head for a moment. "I won lots of races till I got hurt, and had lots of buddies in the Kennels." Hunk wasn't sure what the Kennels were, but he listened intently. "I remember you coming to the Track where I was after the accident, and I remember you being nice to me," Henry said. "You didn't have to be, you just were. So, in return, I'll try to leave the Cats alone for you. You think that if I eat one, we'll get sent *off* or *away*, and I'll trust that you're right."

Hunk said nothing. The New Lady had shushed them and left the room, turning out the lights as she went. Hunk laid his head down on his paws and listened for Henry's panting.

"You're my Brother too, Henry," he said finally, then drifted off to sleep.

"Well? Come on you two!" The New Lady tugged at Hunk's leash and brought him back from his memories. He followed her and Henry out the door and into the night. The Robert was waiting, and he took Hunk's leash. The four of them waited for what seemed like forever to Hunk, until finally a car pulled up into the driveway.

The cheeseburger-smelling lady and the man were back, with another man as well. They got out of the car and the woman immediately knelt in front of Hunk. "Hello, beautiful boy," she murmured as she kissed the top of his head. Hunk pulled his head out of her hands and looked back at the Robert. To his horror, he noticed that the Robert had given his leash to this new woman. Where was she taking him? Was this the New Home? Hunk tugged a moment on his leash, straining to go back to the Robert.

The Robert knelt down and took Hunk's head in his hands. "Now, now boy, it's gonna be all right," he said. Hunk's heart slowed a bit, but the woman still had his leash. "This is your new Momma," the Robert said, "and she loves you more than anything and is going to take such good care of you! But, I want you to know, that if you ever need ANYTHING you just call me and I'll come get you. I promise." He rubbed Hunk's head and then stood up. Hunk looked around to see Henry already in the back seat of the car with the man.

"Come on, Hunk!" Henry barked. "This is Scott and he smells like hamburger! Let's go to the New Home!" Hunk tugged toward the car, then looked back at the woman holding his leash. She was hugging the New Lady tightly, tears running down her cheeks.

"Thank you so much," she said to the New Lady, whose beautiful big eyes shone in the moonlight with just a trace of tears. Hunk was loaded into the back seat with Henry and Scott, but quickly turned around to see the New Lady and the Robert waving good-bye to them.

"Good-bye, New Lady!" he yelled. "Take care of Cleo and Angel and Sunshine and Stubby and Dolly...." He had met the New Lady's hounds that week, and had become as friendly with the girls as Angel, the lone male, would let him. "Oh! Take care of Jeany too...she's still in the Dark Place and she's awfully scared!!!"

Soon Hunk and Henry settled into the seats in the car with Scott, and Henry fell asleep. As Hunk shut his eyes, his thoughts first settled on that image of his father. *I promise, Daddy, that I'll be Proud, just like you told me*, he thought. Then came a fleeting image of Jeany, in the Dark Place, crying as he and Henry left her. *Don't worry, Jeany*, Hunk thought, *you'll have a New Home soon, too. The New Lady will take care of you*. Lastly, his thoughts drifted further back into his memory. A beautiful red brindle dog entered his mind...a red brindle with a white ring around his neck and the flattest feet Hunk had ever seen.

I will see you again, Marky. I promise," Hunk thought. *I've always made it back to you before, and I will again.* With that, Hunk snuggled against Scott and drifted off to sleep.

Hunk and Henry entered a new world that night, but they were too tired to remember it. The next day Hunk awoke to the woman coming downstairs into the basement where they were crated, saying his name.

"Hunk? Henry? Wake up, boys, it's time for breakfast," she said. Hunk thought her voice sounded like the Nice Lady's at first, and he didn't know where he was for a moment. Henry, grunting in the crate next to him, brought him back to reality, and he peered out through the crate door at the woman. "Hi there, beautiful!" she said to him. He smiled at her. *She can't be all bad if she thinks I'm beautiful and brings me food!* She opened the crate door and let him out into the yard, along with Henry, as the man fixed their food.

This became a routine for the boys, and they soon learned to call the woman Mommy and the man Scott or Daddy. Hunk was very happy, as well as proud of Henry for keeping his promise about the cats.

One Friday evening, Mommy came down to the basement and let Hunk and Henry out so that she could talk to them. "Now boys," she said, "we've got a big surprise for you. You're going to have a new sister coming to live with you—another greyhound just like you." Hunk wasn't sure what all those words meant, but thought he would just ask Henry later. Henry was very smart. "Daddy's going to get her tomorrow," Mommy said.

Hunk walked over to her and put his head against her shoulder. She always smelled good, and sometimes he could get his nose up into her hair and pretend he was still with the Nice Lady...though his memories of her were fading daily. Mommy scratched Hunk on the head. "You'll always be my first babies, though," Mommy said, her eyes filling with tears. Hunk had noticed that Mommy's eyes did that a lot, especially when she talked about him. He licked her face.

The next day, Daddy didn't let the boys

out as he normally did. Instead, after he fed them, he put them back in their crates, told them to be good boys, and left. Hunk settled down for a nap, only to be interrupted by Henry in the crate next to his.

"Here, kitty-kitty-kitty?" Henry called carefully. One of Mommy's cats, Zooey, had been left in the basement. "Over here, kitty...that's right." Henry urged the cat closer.

"What are you doing?" Hunk asked indignantly.

Henry hushed immediately. "Nothing," he stammered, "only trying to make friends with that beast, is all." Zooey flitted past Hunk's crate and then stopped in front of Henry's, sat down, and began washing his paws. Henry seemed to Hunk to go insane for a moment: he screamed and barked and flung himself at the crate door as though his weight alone would pop the lock and open the crate. Zooey merely stared back at Henry, as though he knew Henry couldn't get out of the crate.

Hunk laughed. "You got to do better than that if you don't want Mommy and Daddy mad at you."

"They wouldn't be mad. At least Daddy wouldn't. Who cares what Mommy thinks— she likes you best anyway," Henry said, scowling. He turned around three times and then settled down into his bedding. "Besides, they're bringing a new one today anyway, so they won't be paying as close attention to me as they will to the new kid."

Hunk was mortified. "Henry, please leave the cats alone. I don't want to go *away* again. I like it here. And Mommy loves you just as much as she does me, I know she does," he said, his voice quivering with fear. Henry did not reply, but fixed his gaze on the cat. "Look, that thing's got a name, just like we do," Hunk said. "Hey! Cat! What's your name?" he asked.

Zooey rolled his eyes over to look at Hunk. "My name is Zooey, what's yours? And what are you, if I might ask? You look rather like deer, though I know that Mommy said she and Scott were bringing home dogs...though I can't imagine why, when they already have us."

Us? Hunk thought. *How many of them are there?* He had only seen Zooey and a brief glimpse of something orange scurrying away.

"I'm Hunk, and this is Henry," Hunk said. "We're greyhounds, not dogs." He seemed pleased with his knowledge until he noticed that both Zooey and Henry were smirking.

"Greyhounds ARE dogs, you doofus," Zooey said as he stood and headed back for the stairs. Hunk sighed loudly and rested his chin on his front paws.

"Okay, fine," Hunk said to Henry when he was sure that Zooey was out of earshot. "Don't make friends with them; they're rude. But don't eat them, okay? Please?"

Henry sighed. "All right, Hunk, I promise I won't eat the cats," he said, adding quietly, "today."

Soon Scott came back home. Hunk and Henry had fallen asleep in their crates when he came in the door. "Get up, boys, and meet your new sister," he said. Hunk shook his head to clear it as he stood. *Great,* he thought. *A girl! I wonder if she talks as much as...what was her name?* An image of the little fawn girl in the Dark Place danced across his memory, then disappeared. Hunk followed Henry out the door and into the yard.

There stood Jeany. Hunk could hardly believe it. Henry had already run over to sniff her dubiously, then barked in her ear to remind her that he was the boss. She looked around the yard with wide eyes, as though she couldn't believe what she was seeing. Hunk ran over to her happily, dancing around her and beckoning her to play.

"I think I want to go inside now please," she said in a quiet voice. What was wrong with her? Hunk nudged her with his nose, but all she did was head back to Scott and lean on him. Hunk cocked his head to one side, watching Scott lead her inside. He ran to the glass door in time to see Scott open a crate and let her in. She at once went to the back of the crate and curled up, still looking wide-eyed and frightened. Hunk ran over to Henry, who was eyeballing a cat on the other side of the fence.

"What's up with her?" Hunk asked.

"Who?" Henry was only halfway paying attention to Hunk, as he marked every move the cat made.

"The fawn girl. I can't remember her

name, but she was at the Dark Place with us, remember?"

"Yeah, yeah, I don't know, why don't you go find out?" Henry said dismissively. Hunk headed back to the door to find Scott sitting outside.

"So, how do you like your new sister, Hunk?" Scott said, rubbing Hunk's ears. Hunk whined and pawed at the door to be let in. "Wanna go see her? Okay, boy," he said, standing up and opening the door. Hunk dashed in and over to Jeany's crate.

"What's wrong?" he asked in a worried tone.

"Who are you?" she asked loudly. "Why are you following me? Leave me alone!" Her huge brown eyes pleaded with Scott, who seemed to understand and pulled Hunk back.

"There now, easy boy, don't frighten her," Scott said. Hunk looked back and discovered to his horror that Scott was coming for him with a muzzle. Hunk wiggled and tried to evade the plastic thing, but to no avail. "Now then, I can let her out," he said.

"No-no-no-no-no-no-no!!" Jeany wailed,

but Scott opened the crate door anyway. "Fine, I still won't come out," she said, remaining in the back of the crate. Just then the door to the yard opened and Mommy walked in, immediately scratching Hunk on the head.

"Well?" she asked Scott. "Did you get her?"

"Yep," Scott replied, "but I think she's spooked or something. She won't come out of the crate." Mommy knelt down and pushed Hunk to the side.

"Not now, precious boy," she said, staring intently into the crate. Jeany stared back defiantly. "Come on out here, girl, I won't hurt you," Mommy said in the same voice she used when she stroked Hunk's ears and called him Beautiful. Jeany cocked her head to one side and studied Mommy for a moment, then stood and came out of the crate. She walked slowly over to Mommy and leaned her head on Mommy's shoulder.

"I didn't want to leave the Track," Jeany sobbed into Mommy's shoulder. "I liked running and chasing the bunny and my sisters and brother were there and I miss them and

these boys are not nice...and I was so scared at
the Dark Place!" Mommy, obviously not
understanding Jeany, simply rubbed Jeany's
ears and kissed her on the head.

"You're going to be fine, sweetie-girl,"
Mommy said. "You're here with us now, and
you're not ever leaving. We'll take good care
of you, just like we do your brothers, Hunk
and Henry." Jeany nuzzled in closer to
Mommy, still whining a bit. "She's just
nervous," Mommy told Scott, who nodded.

Hunk looked at Jeany. She was awfully
close to Mommy. He felt a strange sensation
in his tummy, almost like he was hungry, but
not quite. Every time he heard Mommy tell
Jeany how pretty she was or call Jeany "sweetie
girl" or "Jeany-Bean," he noticed that the pang
in his tummy got worse. Why didn't Jeany
remember them? Why was she suddenly so
sad? Hunk wondered if something had
happened at the Dark Place that frightened her.
Surely the New Lady (whom Mommy was
teaching him to call Kim) wouldn't let that
happen, would she? Why was Mommy paying
so much attention to Jeany? Hunk tried to scoot

in between them.

"Yes, Hunkabuncha, you're still my baby," she said, scratching his ears. "We just have to make Jeany feel at home, is all." Hunk licked Jeany's nose.

"Yuck," she replied, showing him her teeth. "Don't do that again."

Hunk hung his head, and slowly went to one of the dog beds in the middle of the floor. He laid down and sighed loudly. *Things will never be the same now,* he thought. *Mommy and Daddy will be busy with this one, and it will be up to me to make sure Henry leaves the cats alone.* He closed his eyes for a nap.

Later that evening, while Henry was out with Scott, Hunk got a chance to talk to Jeany. He tried to stick his long nose through the air holes in the side of his crate and into hers, but she saw him and showed her teeth again.

"Quit it," she said. "I'm trying to digest that food. At least this stuff tastes better than the other stuff," she said, her sentence trailing off.

"What other stuff?" Hunk asked. "And Jeany, why don't you remember me? Henry and I, we rode up from Home together with you, remember?" He cocked his head to one side. "And Mommy and Scott came and got us, then went back and got you, from the Dark Place."

Jeany's eyes suddenly met his. "They didn't just go back and get me, lamebrain! You've been here a long time. I was there almost as long as I was at any of the Tracks...and it was dark, and I was alone." She sniffed, licking her nose. "I do remember you. I remember you left me." She settled down into her crate, resting her head on her tiny white-tipped paws.

Hunk withdrew his nose with a sigh. How long had he been with Mommy and Scott? Jeany must have been terrified! He felt another odd feeling in his tummy—not the same as when Jeany cuddled with Mommy, but similar and definitely unpleasant. Once again, he settled in to nap.

The days rather ran one into another for Hunk, as his only way of telling time was by following the Routine: food, out, play, crate, sleep, food, out, Upstairs, play, crate, sleep.

His favorite part was the Upstairs time with Mommy and Scott and Henry and Jeany, even though he still had to wear his muzzle. He had tried to tell Mommy that it was only Henry that wanted to eat the cats, but she didn't seem to understand him. Henry understood him, though, and would be angry with him for "exposing the plan." Jeany didn't want to have anything to do with "the plan" or the cats, but she really must have hated having to sleep downstairs in the crates because every night she would scream and cry.

Henry grew increasingly angry and irritable. He even snapped at Hunk one day over a treat. Hunk tried to talk to him about what was wrong, but Henry just told him to mind his own Tail and leave him alone. Hunk was very sad about the way Henry was behaving; but he was becoming a really good friend to Jeany, so he didn't mind too much. She seemed to feel safer when she was with him, and would often nap on, under or near him.

One night, however, everything changed for Hunk. Henry had been holding back as long as he could about the cats, and finally he could stand it no longer. That night, the whole family was Upstairs, and Henry was on the sofa opposite Mommy. Hunk was on the sofa with Mommy, and was snoozing when Mills darted past Henry. Mills was always running past them and Jeany chased him a few times, but most of the time Hunk just ignored him.

What Hunk didn't know was that every time Mills darted past Henry, it hurt Henry in his tummy. He wanted to catch and eat the little orange creature, but he loved Scott so much and wanted so much to make Scott happy that he tried to ignore Mills. Tonight, however, he couldn't ignore Mills any longer. The aching in his tummy had grown until his entire body felt like it was in pain, like the time he caught the lure at the track and it zapped him. Mills ran past his nose, and Henry saw his opportunity.

Henry leapt from the couch and pounced neatly onto Mills. He held the squirming orange cat between his front paws and tried to get his teeth into it so he could give it a good shake. He had to work fast, before...

"HENRY, NO!" yelled Scott.

Henry paused for just a moment, and it was just long enough for Mills to wiggle out from under Henry's paws and dart for the kitchen counter. Henry sprang into the air to follow, but was stopped in midair by Scott's firm grasp on his collar.

Hunk's eyes flew open at the sound of Scott screaming, and felt himself nearly shoved off the sofa as Mommy jumped up to chase Mills. "What's going on?" he whined, as Jeany came running out from the bedroom. "What happened? Where is Scott taking Henry and why is he yelling?" Mommy came back to Hunk momentarily, but only long enough to get him and Jeany by their collars and drag them to the bedroom. The Gate went up and Mommy ran back to the den.

Hunk raised his ears as high as he could and listened, but all he could hear was Mommy crying. Scott was somewhere down in the basement with Henry. Henry! What had happened to Henry?

"Daddy took Henry away," Jeany sniffed. "Everybody's mad! Why? Are they going to send us away too?" Her brown eyes filled with fear as she moved closer to Hunk. "I don't want to go away!"

Hunk licked her nose. "You're not going *away*," he said softly. "We're Petted Out now, and they can't send us away again. I heard Mommy say so." He strained to hear what was going on, but he heard nothing from the basement, Scott, or Henry. Mommy was telling Mills that he was a good boy, and that it would be all right...and then, to Hunk's horror, he heard Mommy tell Mills that it would never happen again. What did that mean? It gave Hunk a funny and sort of frightened feeling in his tummy, and all he wanted right then was to see Henry. He barked slightly, not wanting to make Mommy angry with him but to remind her that he and Jeany were in the bedroom.

"Hush you two!" she said sharply. Hunk hung his head. What was going on? He nudged Jeany, then headed to the corner.

"Let's try to nap a bit," he said. "Mommy will get us when it's time for bed, and maybe she won't yell at us if we're quiet." Jeany just stared at him, then stared back over the Gate and started calling for Scott. Hunk scooted over to her and grabbed at her collar with his teeth. "Stop being a baby," he said. "They will take you away if you don't behave!" Reluctantly, she followed Hunk to the corner and curled up next to him, crying softly.

Hunk was awakened several hours later to Mommy speaking softly in his ear. He opened his eyes and she was lying on the floor next to him, rubbing his ears. Jeany was gone, and Scott was getting into bed. Hunk panicked. Where was Jeany?

Mommy rubbed his head. "Ssssh, Hunkabuncha, it's all right," she said. Her voice sounded funny, and her face smelled like salty tears. "I have to tell you something," she said. "Henry is going to go live with another family soon..." Mommy stopped talking and started making an awful choking sound, and her eyes filled up with tears like the day she and Scott picked them up. "He's going to go live somewhere without cats, because they make him too upset."

Hunk's eyes grew wide. They were sending Henry away. His heart hurt, like he'd eaten too much dinner. He licked Mommy's face, hoping against hope that he wouldn't be next.

As if she had read his mind, the Mommy continued speaking. "Now, don't you worry, my precious one. You're not going anywhere, and neither is your sister Jeany. I just hope you can forgive me for sending your brother away." She started making the awful sound again, and Hunk thought his heart would break. He licked her face again, and tried to tell her that it was okay, but at the same time he felt something new: he WAS angry that Henry was leaving. *Henry is my brother*, he thought...*my brother...but wait a minute*. An image flitted across his mind, of another brindle dog with a white ring around his neck and the flattest feet Hunk had ever seen. He shook his head to clear it, and snuggled close to Mommy until she stood up to take him to his crate.

Henry went away, and soon Hunk forgot how sad he was to see Henry go. He got to see Henry occasionally when he and Mommy would go to Kim's house, because Henry was staying there until he found his Family. Henry didn't really remember Hunk, but he remembered Mommy, and it always made Hunk a little sad when they would leave and he could hear Henry crying for Mommy not to leave him this time.

Mommy and Scott soon started bringing other dogs home, but they were only visiting, like Henry was with Kim. The first one was called Foxfire, and she was only visiting for a few days. Hunk didn't like her because she wasn't very friendly to him and she was noisy. Jeany told him later that Foxi was very upset. Three days after she came to stay with them, Foxi went with Hunk and Jeany to a "Reunion," where lots of other greyhounds were playing and running in a field.

This was like Turn-Out at...at...Hunk couldn't remember what the place was called, but it was like Turn-Out time. It seemed to Hunk that there were thousands of other greyhounds there, all running and playing. This was heaven! Foxi quickly moved away from Mommy and Scott and found a sunny spot in the grass. Hunk was looking for a place to stretch out when Jeany came streaking toward him, obvious terror on her face.

"Hunk! Hunk! Hunk!" she cried, nearly knocking him down as she ran up to him. "It's the person from the Dark Place! They're sending us back!" she cried. Hunk cocked his head to one side, staring at her.

"No one is sending us anywhere, silly," he said, but at the same time he noticed that the person from the Dark Place was indeed there, and she was leading three greyhounds into the yard. "Look, Jeany, she's got others with her," he said. "Remember? The Nice Lady brought us here, and then we stayed at the Dark Place until Mommy and Scott..."

"Mommy and Daddy," Jeany corrected him.

"Whatever," Hunk said, annoyed slightly. "Maybe those three are here to find Mommies and Daddies, huh?" He strained his eyes to get a better look. He KNEW those dogs! Striper, Diesel, and Luna had all been at the...at...HOME, that's what it was! They had all been at Home with him and...Hunk knotted his brow a moment, trying to remember the name of the dog with the flat feet.

"Hey, that red one is handsome," Jeany whispered. "Wasn't he at the Farm with us?" She licked her nose and tried valiantly to get the muzzle to come loose from her head. "How am I going to get his attention if I have this ridiculous thing on my face?"

"His name is Striper," Hunk said. "And if you figure out how to get that thing off, let me know, will ya?" He stopped talking to her long enough to scrub his face in the grass, trying to pull the awful green muzzle off. Jeany took the opportunity to flit across the field to Striper.

"Fosters," as Mommy called them, came and went. Foxi met her new humans at the "Reunion". Henry came back for a short time, but it wasn't the same. He was angry with Mommy and determined not to get attached to Scott again, so he stayed in his crate most of the time, even when Scott would leave the door open. Striper came and went, and was followed by other dogs. Profile, the big white and brindle male, came for a month and then left. Xena, the biggest girl that Hunk had ever seen, frolicked about the yard for a few months and then left. Hunk was starting to understand what this "foster" thing meant. It was sort of like his time at the Tracks, coming and going and never staying anywhere for long.

Hunk was glad he wasn't a "foster" anymore, and made sure to thank Mommy by licking her face every time he got a chance. She called him her Hunkabunchalove, and Hunk and Jeany were quite happy in their little family. He still held his head high, and still acted like the Proud Racer he had been. He had finally learned the true rewards for being a Proud Racer...living in this home, being with Mommy and Scott, and having Jeany for a Sister. Hunk thought now and then of Marky, hoping that his brother had also discovered the secret—that Marky had also found the reward of truly being Home.

The Author wishes to thank...

Scott—my partner and my husband: for your support and encouragement, for letting me sleep while you feed the howling masses, and for convincing me that greyhounds were the breed for us.

My family—Hoyt and Martha Allen, and Susan and Dave Allen Grady: for supporting my writing habit and loving me despite my bizarre fascination with all things long-legged and needle-nosed...and for raising me to believe that all creatures are reflections of the Divine.

Jeany, Bo, Profile, and Liz—my darling hounds: for teaching me about unconditional love, greyhound hugs, and how to be lost for hours in a stunning pair of brown eyes.

Greyhound Crossroads: for blessing me and trusting me with the precious gift of my five miraculous hounds.

All my foster dogs and their families: for teaching me how much I love to watch that moment when a dog picks his or her human.

And lastly—my Hunkamuncha from Oz: you are the inspiration for my greyhound adoption work...and my best friend. I wish everyone could have a heart dog like you...and I am thankful every day that you walked over to ME that first day we met. You are the most precious, funny, irritating, maddening, amazing, strong, shy, and miraculous creature I have ever known. Thanks for letting me be your Mommy.

Hunk and his Mommy

L-R Hunk, Jeany, Liz, Profile...
Nancy is the one getting licked. :)